the Flowers of Eve

Christiana Gagen

All rights reserved
Copyright © January 1994 Christiana Gagen
Cover design by Kingwood Creations
This book or any portion thereof may not be reproduced or used in any manner whatsoever without the express written permission of the author except for the use of brief quotations in a book review.
ISBN: 9798218005955

> Trigger warning: although written by a minor this work contains mentions of self-harm, suicidal ideation, and domestic violence.

For Deanna

*the flowers of Eve
are the first of their kind
the stories they weave
I've left behind*

Contents

time 13

mr. sun 15

fire hazard 17

A/C (Alternating Current) 19

He Says 20

simpleton 23

Precipitation 25

Prism 27

(untitled) 29

To You 31

I like him 33

The Blonde Man 37

the Pretender 39

the man in black 40

I Know An Asshole 43

fear 45

alone 47

contentment or isolation 49

time

time is drifting away
there is not time to have anything to say.
we hear the phrase "i don't have enough time to stay."
and we go on every day.
we all seem to be drifting apart,
it seems we don't take this to heart.
i don't see why we're all so stressed,
i don't see why we haven't all confessed.
what is there to get so worked up about, time goes by, we can't do anything to stop time so why try?
unplanned things will come up so have some time aside,
just don't make your schedule too "tight."
we are born and we die,
we say hello and goodbye.
i don't see why we choose to get "worked up,"
we get so upset like we're going to erupt.
who will have time to read this?
we hardly have time for a goodbye kiss.
there are 24 hours in a day,
60 minutes to each hour,
60 seconds to each minute,
why is that such a hard concept to grasp?
why are so many of us so unorganized?
i want to sit and philosophize.
seems we can't make time anymore,
knew a friend who cared said "i tried making

time dear, but i can't."
so time is money,
i think it's funny,
so many of us run around like dummies.
make money, make money, faster, faster,
surprise, disaster!
it all crashed and they say let's put it back with plaster.
i say chuck it all, before or after the fall.

mr. sun

i hate you mr. sun,
i hate when you ruin my fun.
go away mr. sun,
the day is done.
mr. sun get away from me,
mr. sun you made me not see.
i can't ever recall liking you,
i can't recall you making anything look new.
you make everything bright,
that's why i like the night.
you know the purpose of space,
is to get a big pencil, get close to you, and erase!
i don't care if you make everything grow,
i don't care if everything would be dead.
i'd rather the sky be black as crow,
i'd rather think clearly in my head.
so i'll spend the rest of my life,
trying to find a way to keep you out of the sky.
could i cut you out with a knife?
then you would disappear and everything
would die.

fire hazard

i am a fire hazard
please step around me.
all the adults tell me,
i'm against some ordinance code,
but all the kids want me around.
yes i am a fire hazard
if there was a fire,
everyone running for their lives,
do you really think i'd get in the way?
look i AM a fire hazard
just jump over me.
don't tell me i'm clutter, paper, or old furniture,
i am a fire hazard that's all ok?
see this fire hazard
this is me.
i don't really get in the way
there probably won't be a fire anyway.
i chose to be a fire hazard
ignore me.
if i wasn't what would i be?
i know!   a malcontent creep.

A/C (Alternating Current)

he holds his Love
and throws it against the wall.
he rises above
and takes his greatest fall.
he flies like a dove
and reaches his master's call.
he catches her in a glove
and Loves her like she is a doll.
he speaks, they speak of,
and has hatred towards all.

He

"It's love" he says,
"It's forever" he says,
"I'll do anything" he says,
"You just need some time" he says,
"I'll give you a few days" he says,
"Don't end it now" he says,
"Come back and work it out" he says,
"We will be together" he says,
"I've changed" he says,
"He doesn't love you" he says,
"He can't remember your name" he says,
"I'm not finished talking" he says,
"You will listen to me" he says,
"I won't hurt you" he says,
"I'm only being firm" he says,
"I really love you" he says,

Says
it's abuse,
it's a ruse.
he's a liar,
he tires.
i want out,
i don't doubt.
i lock the door,
i don't want him anymore.
i flinch,
my fists clench.
no one to call,
up against the wall.
struggle to be free,
struggle hopelessly.
bruises on my wrists,
run away and resist.

simpleton

the way you are, the way you act,
you make me sick and that is a fact.
you come to my window, wait until i wake,
i tell you to go, and the truth i tell you, you say is fake.
hey, i do not want to see you today
hey, if it is june i do not want to see you until may
hey, i do not care what you have to say
hey, it is time to pay.
pay for all the shit you tell me
i do not want you i care about andy.
you say you will leave us alone
later you call on the phone.
the way we were is gone forever
also the nights when we were together.
if i rolled away you would pull me back and hold me down,
i am glad you are gone
because you always fucked around.
before if you wanted me to sit in a chair,
you made sure i didn't move from there.
you say you, still love me,
but you do not care how i feel.
if you did, you would care more about me than yourself,
do you not know that liars burn in hell?

---

you can not change me
no matter what you do
i think i will always hate you.

Precipitation

& when the rain falls, i fall too,
hitting the ground to shatter.
i am a tear, but won't shed one for you,
being away so long, do i matter?
missing you becomes my mood,
this heartache into my personality.
the solutions and answers elude,
i don't know if going on is a possibility.
i want all or nothing,
i want to Love or die.
it is isolation or touching?
will i tell the truth or lie?
do i care to surrender or fight?
is the pain physical or emotional?
am i in darkness or light?
should i leave you in silence or call?
loving so long is not hard,
not when it's the only thing.
only thing not marred,
to my darkness i cling.
here i lay, put a glance on my grave.
no more i can say, i can face it but i'm not brave.
started burying myself from the inside,
killing and numbing the pain i let you give me.
breaking my own heart, in you i want to confide,
others wish to be normal, i wish not to be.

standing alone or standing with you, they all tell me to move on.
maybe stupidity but i'll stay true.

Prism

the only excuse,
is i'm not here,
i already forgave you for anything,
& i can't find you dear.
why did you go?
so i couldn't find?
forgiveness too much?
another chance, will you be so kind?
searching through empty faces,
& one contact.
not finding any traces,
our separation a fact.
depression is the only thing,
loneliness & who i am.
come again and sing,
that wasn't a sham.
black is only a symbol,
the rain my happiness.
maybe an absence of color,
no tears i confess.
blue is numb comfort,
purple is social and ready.
green i am ready to flirt,
grey is softness not like a teddy.

(untitled)

there he stands
and i try to keep my head above the sea
i watch him sing
i watch him scream
and i wonder if there are others staring,
as transfixed as me?
he gets me so excited almost falling down
but i keep my eyes on him
and then it's over.
he says thank you as he walks away
clad in leather, offstage
i clutch the tags around my neck
hope to see him later
but will he be gone again?
like he was in hawaii?
Lance followed him to the hotel
asking about a love song
he told he'd loved and they had gone away
pale face in moonlight.
i make my way
guided by people who show distaste
or are afraid.
i find the place
am alone
sitting down,
it is not silent
and i wait for the man
who has become
more than nothing.

To You

i just wanted to tell you i'm not worth anything,
i'm worthless.
no i'm not special
& there's nothing wrong.
yeah i wrote that note
to get you to go away
so you wouldn't think i was someone
yeah just go away.
i don't want any comfort
or soothing empathy.
just nothing in this cold black void
yeah HOLE
only here, power
blue, black, silver
it was my choice
creation.
it sounds depressing
it looks confused
it smells lost
it's a smooth lake
almost a mirror of me.
& the meaning i still can't see.
i can't stop here
this is too dear
i want the height,
the view and the sight.
the gravity, & i'll be,
nothing!
fall fall falling

only before stalling.
i didn't change my mind,
the memories i didn't find.
this way i chose,
to bring my life to a close.
'cause there's no stopping,
all it takes is a little hopping.
you get a great adrenaline rush,
hardly pain before you're mush.
it's my way of dying,
sensation of flying.
maybe i'll see god in heaven,
maybe i'll burn in hell,
this flight will tell.
sorry for the obsession,
good bye kevin.
my only fear you'll follow me,
only fear you care too deeply.
i didn't want to mean anything to you
wanted to drift apart,
didn't want you to Love me too,
didn't want to hurt your heart.

I like him

softly, calmly
he walks with ease and grace.
does he see me,
if he notices there's no trace.
maybe he is not perfect
body or face.
but i follow him from place
to place.
anger eludes him
calmness in him.
funny to be,
beside an obsession.
especially when
they're oblivious.
mind goes blank
of anything to say.
fragments and
ideas of thoughts.
grace, calmness, resplendent, silent, figment,
words to describe him.
paint a picture of perfect grace,
i look closely to see his face.
lovely idea
obsolete and unique.
there is no clone
him alone.
this bird has flown
to his window sill,
watch enough to fulfill.

we do not chase
after Love,
if anything lust.
not even
something unknown.
stare inside
to see surprise.
is it physical?
if he touched
you there what
would you feel?
would you be
turned on?
or is it all
mental?
every night
leave a single feather

on his glove
of leather.
when it's dark,
and he's vanished.
step through threshold
silence, blindness, black on black,
a finger through private possession
when it's dark
and he's vanished.
secrets to steal.
privacy to violate.
creep away before it's too late.
flutter outside,
perch in a corner,
successfully hide.
good not to be friends,
keep a secret to lie.
an overheard conversation,
many a time.
an open window while on the phone.
a hidden camera's quiet click.
a lost note taken.
an unknown stalker.
collected day by day,
over a year.
the information a right to call it stolen?
or has an idea or dream,
gone too far?
drive away unliked chances,
he hasn't the right for romances,
i am the one who pulls his puppet strings.

The Blonde Man
he's gone now
he'll take so many with him
sometimes i confuse him with
another blond man
some are insulted, but why?
i Loved them both and
both are gone now.
one forever
and one just from my life.
just names carved into my skin,
just a memory,
just ashes,
just life and love gone
forever?they said take some time,
not some pills
you'll go on.
it's been a year and two months,
it's been three months.
it still hurts,
you still haunt my dreams,
one or the other,
sometimes i don't know which.
i see you walking,
from the cliff
but by the time i climb down
i wake up.
you're gone now,
both of you.
i couldn't have one or the other,

i had to have both or neither.
gone now.

come again blond man,
i don't know, who are you?
are you real?
or are you both,
illusions in my mind.
take the silence,
in a dream,
take me too,
i want to leave.
i want the blond man,
& have my blond man come too.
you're such a mystery
that figment,
that form,
in my mind,
dancing in my vision,
not there when i reach,
fall down hopelessly.
away and alone,
shaking.
i want to cry,
it hurts too much,
and i can't lie.

the Pretender

he pretends he's violent
that he's the dominator
problem being i believed
what he said and not what i felt
never understood how shy
how insecure, what the ideals
never understood where he was coming from,
& what he was trying to say,
then again he never knew me or how deep my pain
couldn't stay together
so how should it end?
i don't want to pretend.
everyone believes my lies
& calls me a liar when i tell the truth
& so did the pretender
to the last word, the last lie i told.
i didn't want to ever lie
but who can trust a creep?
& a malcontent creep as i am?
why does it always end this way?
in anger when i try to tell the truth.
but he lied too or just doesn't know what Love is.
& when i have Love i throw it away.
first time didn't know it, told him to go away
now i'm screaming his name.

the man in black

the darkness is his blanket,
but he's not afraid of the light.
i was drawn to him on sight,
he can erase me anytime.
if they push him around,
they're going to get torn down.
you can't push him too far
'cause he's ready to die.
don't be afraid, he only lashes out once in a while,
it's just blood is his style.
oh he's got a sense of humor all right,
his kiss is a cut,
that caress like a knife,
he'll hurt you if you smile.

i wondered how that mind thought
if he would let me push the hair away if it was dark.
yeah, i even wondered how those lips would kiss.
so he said what he thought
& i thought he looked nice.
i could tell there was no fat under the black.
he stretched out his arms and they stayed that way,
i stepped into them and they surrounded me, stopped breathing to believe.
he offered first, further contact.
& we went away
two days we spoke again
said we'd write letters
i found out about her.
i'm still infatuated, i can stand criticism
i can stand being lashed out at, the blood shows his love.
ok, so we're far away, the words make it ok.

I Know An Asshole

I know an asshole,
his name is Chad,
he thinks he's bad.
I know an asshole,
he wants to get fucked all the time,
his girlfriend thinks that's just fine,
too bad she's not there all the time.
I know an asshole,
he thinks he's funny,
i think he's loony.
I know an asshole,
he says "you take me too serious"
hmmm? Try delirious.
I know an asshole,
he's really nice i was told,
he's too damn bold.
I know an asshole,
he looks like a jock,
i think he should fuck off.

fear

i used to sleep at night
all darkness, no trace of light
then he came and brought such fright
i looked, i turned and ran, he was mutilated
i tried to scream at his sight.
i was running because, because
the man standing aside kept saying how great
the other was
he'll kill only with his bare hands
no reason, just does.
i turned and looked into eyes as red as blood
then i was sinking in a pool of mud
i was sinking in the middle of a flood.
i kept thinking how harsh he'd kill, and not with
a gun
crush me with mere strength, his fun
when would this be done
who would be the one to say, i won?
where, is the sun?
i awoke warm and wet,
i was trembling and yet
i wondered what was next.
such fear had been brought to me
to it all what was the key?
did i tremble with fright
and could i pretend it was glee?

alone

anger, feel it inside,
feel it twist and writhe,
when it finds,
it's way out, i make sure to be alone.
when it's gone, only marks left,
on my arms and mind.
shaking always on the inside,
sometimes on the outside.
physical pain is a distraction
i don't even think about.
red marks on my arms, they go away,
in more than a day.
shaking, goes away,
in less than an hour.
the nightmares, maybe never.
cold sweat can be,
washed or wiped off.
twitching, usually,
stops.
but in my mind, the thoughts,
and really, how were you supposed to?
maybe, i am crazy.
i don't expect you to deal with it.
sure, i look okay,
walking up saying hey,
but then listen to what i say.
i can not always keep it at bay,
is that why they eventually all go away?
and do i really have to stay?

contentment or isolation

woke up someday,
looked around my cave.
realized what i had become,
almost undone.
so long all i've wanted to be alone,
get my music in the mail,
long ago i gave up on detail.
forgot why i should eat,
forgot when i should sleep.
stopped taking showers for a long time,
now i know the meaning of grime.
why do i feel so dizzy?
why do i feel like acid is eating my soul?
at least my hair isn't frizzy,
there are no dreams to make me toss and roll.
i don't even think of another try.
too many decisions on food.
too many people will break my heart.
too much time it takes to bathe.
too much sanity to lose to nightmares.
i tried eating but i ran out of money
i tried the social world but there is too much pain.
i tried keeping clean but i don't like to feel that way.
i tried sleeping but the more i tried,
the more nightmares came and took it away.

Acknowledgements

To my friend Anne C, hey girl! Thank you for going on this journey with me. Thank you to Miles for all your love and support. Thank you Deanna for always believing in me.

www.ingramcontent.com/pod-product-compliance
Lightning Source LLC
Chambersburg PA
CBHW032005060426
42449CB00031B/707